CliffsNotes

Hardy's
The Return of the Native

By Frank H. Thompson, Jr., M.A.

University of Nebraska

IN THIS BOOK

- Hardy's Life and Career
- Brief Synopsis of the Novel
- List of Characters
- Chapter Summaries and Commentaries
- Analyses of Main Characters
- Critical Analysis
- Review Questions and Theme Topics
- Selected Bibliography
- Find additional information to further your study online at www.cliffsnotes.com

WILEY

Wiley Publishing, Inc.

Publisher's Acknowledgments

Editor
Gary Carey, M.A., University of Colorado

Consulting Editor
James L. Roberts, Ph.D., Department of
English, University of Nebraska

Production
Wiley Publishing, Inc. Composition Services

CliffsNotes™ *The Return of the Native*

Published by:
Wiley Publishing, Inc.
909 Third Avenue
New York, NY 10022
www.wiley.com

CONTENTS

The Return of the Native

HARDY'S LIFE AND CAREER

Born on June 2, 1840, in Upper Bockhampton, not far from Dorchester, in Dorsetshire, Thomas Hardy was the son of Thomas Hardy, a master mason or building contractor, and Jemima Hand, a woman of some literary interests. Hardy's formal education consisted only of some eight years in local schools, but by the end of this period he had on his own read a good deal in English, French, and Latin, just as later in London he made his own rather careful study of painting and English poetry. He was also interested in music and learned to play the violin. At the age of sixteen he was apprenticed to an architect in Dorchester and remained in that profession, later in London and then again in Dorchester, for almost twenty years.

He began to write poetry during this time, but none of it was published. His first novel, *The Poor Man and the Lady,* written in 1867-68, was never published, and the manuscript did not survive except insofar as Hardy used parts of it in other books. His first published novel was *Desperate Remedies* in 1871; the first novel which came out in serial form before publication as a book, an arrangement he was to follow for the rest of his novels, was *A Pair of Blue Eyes* in 1873; his real fame as a novelist, along with sufficient income to enable him to abandon architecture for good, came with *Far from the Madding Crowd* in 1874. On September 17, 1874, Hardy married Emma Lavinia Gifford.

From this time on Hardy devoted his full time to writing, continuing to publish novels regularly until his last, *Jude the Obscure,* in 1895. Among these are some of the best of his so-called Wessex novels (Hardy uses the name of one of the kingdoms of Anglo-Saxon Britain to designate an area including his native Dorsetshire): *The Return of the Native,* 1878; *The Mayor of Casterbridge,* 1886; *The Woodlanders,* 1887; *Tess of the D'Urbervilles,* 1891; in addition to *Jude.* To this list of best should be added the earlier *Far from the Madding Crowd.*

In writing most of his novels, Hardy meticulously worked out the details of time and geography he wanted to use; almost every novel is, therefore, located in a carefully mapped out area of Wessex and covers a specified period of time. *The Return of the Native,* for example, covers the period 1842-43 in its first five books and is set on Puddletown Heath (called Egdon Heath in the novel), on which Upper Bockhampton is situated. This novel also reveals a side of Hardy's authorship for which he has been taken to task by critics. In response to requests from readers of the novel in serial form, he added a sixth book to the original five to give his story a happier ending. Hardy seems to have responded to the demands of his audience with what must seem like careless indifference nowadays. He says in a note to the novel that the reader can choose which of the two endings he prefers but that the rigorous reader will probably favor the original conception. (For a discussion of the effects on the novel of this addition of a book, see the Commentary for Book Sixth.)

Tess sold more rapidly than any of his other novels, and *Jude* was probably more vehemently denounced. During this period of time Hardy also published his first poems as well as short stories. On June 29, 1885, he moved into a house he had built in Dorchester and lived there for the rest of his life.

On November 27, 1912, Mrs. Hardy died, a woman with whom he had become increasingly incompatible; and on February 10, 1914, he married Florence Emily Dugdale, a woman whom he had referred to for several years previously as his assistant and who was about forty years younger than he. After the appearance of *Jude* Hardy devoted his attention entirely to poetry and drama, publishing a number of books of poems, including one which he prepared just before his death. He also wrote and published an epic drama on the Napoleonic era, *The Dynasts,* which appeared in three parts with a total of nineteen acts. He was given a number of honors, including an honorary degree from Oxford. The success of *Tess* had made possible a good income from his writing for the rest of his life, and when he died he left an estate of nearly half a million dollars. He died on January 11, 1928, and a few days later was buried in Westminster Abbey.

BRIEF SYNOPSIS

Across Egdon Heath on a November day a reddleman is traveling with a young woman whose identity he conceals from a chance acquaintance of the road. The reddleman notices the figure of a woman atop Rainbarrow, the largest of the Celtic burial mounds in the area, and then, replacing her, other figures. These are heath folk come to start a Fifth of November bonfire.

The reddleman, Diggory Venn, returns safely to Mrs. Yeobright her niece, Thomasin Yeobright, who was to have married Damon Wildeve that day. Mrs. Yeobright takes Thomasin with her to see Wildeve at the inn he operates in order to demand an explanation of his failure to marry her. The heath folk, after the bonfire, come to serenade the supposed newlyweds, and when Wildeve is able to get rid of them he starts off to see Eustacia Vye, the mysterious figure Venn saw earlier on the barrow.

Eustacia watches for Wildeve on Rainbarrow, returning now and then to check on the signal fire she has had built before her grandfather's house (Captain Vye is the chance acquaintance of Venn's). Wildeve, who was once her lover but whom she has not seen since his interest in Thomasin, does finally arrive.

Venn accidentally learns of the meeting between Eustacia and Wildeve. The reddleman, a longtime admirer and once rejected suitor of Thomasin, resolves to help her and purposely overhears the conversation the next time Eustacia and Wildeve meet on Rainbarrow. Venn then calls on Eustacia to get her to help Thomasin, finally telling her he knows about her meetings with Wildeve. Venn also informs Mrs. Yeobright he would like to marry her niece. Though he is rejected, the aunt uses him as a means to put pressure on Wildeve. Wildeve goes immediately to Eustacia to convince her to leave with him, but she will not answer right away. The news of the arrival for the Christmas holidays of Mrs. Yeobright's son Clym is widely talked about on the heath, including Captain Vye's house.

Eustacia hears much about Clym, and Mrs. Yeobright and Thomasin make preparations for his arrival. After getting a glimpse of him, Eustacia is fascinated by this native returned from Paris and arranges to substitute for one of the boys in the traditional Christmas mumming, the first performance of which is at a party Mrs. Yeobright is giving. Eustacia succeeds in meeting Clym but while she is in costume. Now that her interest in Wildeve has paled, Eustacia makes clear to Venn that she would like to see Wildeve married to Thomasin. They do marry, with Eustacia serving as witness. Mrs. Yeobright, who has once opposed the marriage, does not attend; and Clym, who has been away from home, finds out about it only after it has taken place.

Giving up his business career in Paris, Clym has returned to Egdon Heath to set up as a schoolteacher to those who can't afford existing schools. Mrs. Yeobright disapproves, thinking Clym is not ambitious enough. Clym meets Eustacia, in her own person this time, and is strongly attracted to her, an attraction that Mrs. Yeobright argues against. He sees Eustacia regularly, usually on the heath, for several months and then asks her to marry him. She says yes, though she hopes he will finally give up his plans and take her to Paris.

When Mrs. Yeobright and Clym quarrel over his love of Eustacia and he feels forced to leave his mother's house, he decides they should marry right away and live for a time on the heath. Clym finds a cottage and moves from home, leaving his mother disconsolate and bitter. Wildeve's interest in Eustacia revives when he hears of her approaching marriage. One the occasion of their marriage, Mrs. Yeobright sends a small inheritance to both Thomasin and Clym, but her handyman loses it gambling with Wildeve, who wants revenge on his wife's aunt for not trusting him with the money. Venn, protecting Thomasin, wins it back from Wildeve, but not understanding that part of it is Clym's, the reddleman delivers it all to Thomasin.

Eustacia and Clym for a time live a secluded life. When Mrs. Yeobright receives no response from Clym about the money, she calls on Eustacia, and they quarrel bitterly. Clym, hurrying his study to be a teacher so as to pacify the impatient Eustacia, develops severe eye trouble and is forced to suspend his work. To his wife's dismay, he takes up furze cutting as a way of making a little money and getting exercise. To Eustacia this is a far cry from what she yearns for: the gay life of the great world, especially as represented by Paris. To compensate, she goes to a gipsying (a dance) and unexpectedly encounters Wildeve and dances with him. Venn sees them together and attempts to discourage Wildeve's loitering around Clym's house at night.

Persuaded by the reddleman to forget her pride and call on her son, Mrs. Yeobright starts the long walk to his house on a hot

August day. She sees Wildeve admitted by Eustacia before she can get there; when she knocks on the door, Clym's wife looks out the window but doesn't answer. The older woman tries to walk back home, stops in exhaustion, and is bitten by an adder. She is later discovered by Clym, who has set off for her house to attempt a reconciliation, but even medical attention cannot save her and she dies. Clym blames himself for her death. Eustacia is nearby when Mrs. Yeobright dies but doesn't make an appearance; she has accidentally encountered Wildeve, who has lately come into an inheritance.

Clym for some time is ill and irrational because of his mother's death. His constant blaming of himself exhausts Eustacia, and she tries to find consolation in Wildeve. Once back to normal again, Clym sets out to discover what his mother was doing on the heath. From Mrs. Yeobright's handyman, Venn, and a young boy who came across his mother as she tried to get home that day, Clym learns what happened. He accuses Eustacia of cruelty to his mother and deception of himself as a husband, and she leaves his house to return to Captain Vye's.

At her grandfather's Eustacia doesn't know how to occupy herself and once even thinks of suicide. A bonfire is lit for her when the Fifth of November comes, an inadvertent signal to Wildeve, who offers to help Eustacia get away from the heath to Paris. On Thomasin's advice Clym, now moved back to his mother's house, writes to ask his wife to return to him.

On the evening of the sixth of November Eustacia signals to Wildeve that she wants to go, by chance not getting Clym's letter before she leaves the house. Thomasin, who has suspicions about Wildeve, and Captain Vye, who finds out Eustacia has left the house very late at night, come to ask Clym's help. As Thomasin tries to get back home, finally with Venn's assistance, as Wildeve waits with a gig for Eustacia, and as Clym looks for his wife, Eustacia on this dark, stormy night throws herself in a stream near a weir. Both Wildeve and Clym try to rescue her, but it is Venn who pulls out both men as well as Eustacia. Of the three only Clym survives.

After her husband's death, Thomasin moves into the family home with Clym. Venn, having given up the reddle trade, calls on her, and they become interested in each other. However, Clym thinks he ought to ask his cousin to marry him, since his mother wished it. But Thomasin and Venn decide to marry and do. Clym is last seen on top of Rainbarrow, performing as an itinerant preacher of moral lectures.

LIST OF CHARACTERS

Clym (Clement) Yeobright

A young man of about thirty who gives up a business career in Paris to return to his native Edgon Heath to become a "schoolmaster to the poor and ignorant."

Eustacia Vye

A young woman of nineteen who is frustrated by life on the heath and who longs for the gay life of the world.

Mrs. Yeobright

Clym's mother, a widow of inflexible standards.

Thomasin (Tamsin) Yeobright

Clym's cousin and Mrs. Yeobright's niece, a young girl of gentle ways and conventional expectations.

Damon Wildeve

An ex-engineer who is keeper of the Quiet Woman Inn, a man easily infatuated by women.

Diggory Venn

A resourceful man of twenty-four and a reddleman (a traveling seller of reddle, red chalk used for marking sheep).

Captain Vye

Eustacia's grandfather and a former sailor.

Timothy Fairway

A pompous, sententious man of middle age who is greatly respected by the other heath folk and who is a furze dealer.

Grandfer Cantle

A somewhat senile and always lively ex-soldier of about sixty-nine.

Christian Cantle

Grandfer Cantle's fearful and timid thirty-one-year-old son.

Humphrey

A furze cutter.

Sam

A turf cutter.

Susan Nunsuch

A woman who suspects that Eustacia is a witch and that she has cast evil spells on her son.

Johnny Nunsuch

Susan's son, a young boy.

Olly Dowden

A besom (heath broom) maker.

Charley

A sixteen-year-old boy who works for Captain Vye and who admires Eustacia, largely from afar.

Summaries and Commentaries

BOOK FIRST

CHAPTERS 1-2

Summary

Near twilight on a Saturday in November Egdon Heath slowly turns dark. It has changed little from the way it was described in ancient times. The only evidence of man's activity is an old highway and an even older barrow.

An old man in clothes of nautical style makes his way along this highway and presently catches up with another traveler walking alongside a van. By the red color of his complexion, his clothes, and his van, the second man is identified as a reddleman. During a desultory conversation, the old man discovers the other has a young woman in his van, but the reddleman will say little about her. He leaves the old man to pull off the road and rest, and while he does so the reddleman sees a figure on top of the highest point in the heath, a Celtic barrow. When it finally leaves its position, he can tell it is a woman, and he is surprised to see her place taken by several other figures.

Commentary

It is significant that Hardy devotes the entire first chapter of his novel to a description of Egdon Heath; even more significant is the way he described it. It is said to be eternally waiting and "unmoved" in its "ancient permanence." The "storm [is] its lover, and the wind its friend." "It [has] a lonely face, suggesting tragical possibilities"; and its characteristic vegetation gives it an "antique brown dress." In short, Hardy gives animation and a personality to Egdon. Some critics have gone so far as to speak of the heath as one of the main characters in the novel, if not the sole main character.

It is perhaps more relevant to think of Egdon Heath as a symbol. Hardy himself suggests that such a "gaunt waste" with its "chastened sublimity" may come to represent a new ideal of beauty for modern man. But this is, of course, an indirect way of commenting on modern man and his view of the universe. It is well to remember that no beings appear in the novel until the second chapter and even then they are not named. At the very least, Egdon is shown to be inhospitable to man, even as it is almost untouched by him.

It is here, then, that the events Hardy sets in motion will play themselves out. When human figures do finally appear, they seem insignificant against the backdrop of the indifferent, if not hostile, Egdon. Many times during the course of the story, for instance, Clym will be shown to appear like a tiny insect moving across the face of nature. The heath as a setting and a symbol as well as the way the first people to appear are shown in relation to their surroundings vividly conveys Hardy's theme in the novel: that man lives his life in a universe that is at least indifferent to him and may be hostile.

Many events to come in the story are foreshadowed in these opening chapters. The fact that the old man is returning to his home and the reddleman is bringing the young woman to hers (these characters are later identified as Captain Vye, Diggory Venn, and Thomasin Yeobright) hints at the more important homecoming of Clym Yeobright in Book Second. Hardy also uses deliberate mystification to presage the future: he raises questions about the reddleman and about the woman on the barrow (Eustacia Vye), and he implies that the young woman in the van is in some kind of difficulty. In fact, without identifying them yet, Hardy has presented most of the main characters about whose future the events of the novel will be concerned.

Hardy has sometimes been accused of inept handling of plot, partly because of his preference for developing his story through a series of short scenes. Such series do often occur in this novel, and it is sometimes distracting to be pulled from one scene to another so quickly, especially with the accompanying shift in point of view. Yet, in chapter 3 occurs one of several long scenes developed in rather great detail. It is true, however, that the short scene gets more frequent use than the long.

CHAPTER 3

Summary

The figures on Rainbarrow, as it is called, are the heath folk come to build the traditional Fifth of November bonfire. The group includes, among others, Timothy Fairway, Grandfer Cantle, Christian Cantle, Humphrey, Sam, Olly Dowden, and Susan Nunsuch. As they watch the fire, they discuss the marriage that day of Thomasin Yeobright, Mrs. Yeobright's niece, and Damon Wildeve, an engineer turned innkeeper, as well as Mrs. Yeobright's earlier disapproval of it. They also mention the imminent arrival of Mrs. Yeobright's son Clym. The bonfire in front of Captain Vye's leads to comments on him and his granddaughter Eustacia. And Christian's ineptness with women comes in for extended discussion. When their fire dies out, Fairway leads the way with Susan Nunsuch in a wild dance through the embers.

The dance is interrupted by the arrival of the reddleman, who inquires the way to Mrs. Yeobright's house. Mrs. Yeobright herself comes by, looking for Olly Dowden, and the two women go off together toward the Quiet Woman Inn, which is now to be Thomasin's home.

Commentary

Of the bonfires lighting up the heath this night, Hardy says that they "are rather the lineal descendants from jumbled Druidical rites and Saxon ceremonies than the invention of popular feeling about Gunpowder Plot." The Gunpowder Plot refers to Guy Fawkes, and Fifth of November is Guy Fawkes Day. Though apparently the custom of observing this day is dying out elsewhere, on Egdon Heath, remote and provincial, it is still observed, along with other traditional or customary practices, as shown later in the novel.

The occasion of the bonfire also gives Hardy the opportunity to show the heath dwellers as not only traditional but also superstitious and prone to believe in folk wisdom. All are willing to ascribe truth to the saying "No moon, no man" as it applies in general as well as in particular to the case of Christian Cantle. They all appear to believe, also, that ghosts do exist (the one mentioned is said to be red) and that they appear only to "single sleepers," like Christian. Not even Fairway, who is looked up to by the others, questions any of these beliefs.

Certainly Christian Cantle's life is dominated by such wisdom and superstition; he says of himself that he is "a man of the mournfullest make." Hardy uses him as a ludicrous figure, a grotesque, who is defined solely by his shortcomings and fears. In him the fears of all the provincials or rustics are given open expression. Grandfer Cantle, Christian's father, is also a grotesque but of a different sort. If Christian is all fear, Grandfer is all self-advertised courage, as in his repeated references here and elsewhere to his service in 1804 as a soldier in the "Bang-up Locals." He is also a parody of senility in his songs and wild jigs. Between these two and the less demonstrative Humphrey and Sam, stands the pompous and sententious Fairway. Father and son are used by Hardy for the purposes of a slapstick humor, but Fairway is deflated as a stuffed shirt, as shown, for example, in the way he is presented in his telling of the tale about Mrs. Yeobright's earlier objections to Thomasin's marriage. Some critics say that Hardy uses this group of minor characters as a kind of chorus, in the manner of a Greek play.

Certainly the conversation and gossip of these characters is used to describe events that have happened in the past, an older technique partly replaced in the modern novel by the flashback. They also comment on events and people in the present as well as look to what will happen in the immediate future. Their opinions are important for Hardy's purposes, since they represent the community in which the main characters live out their lives.

CHAPTERS 4-5

Summary

Outside the inn Mrs. Yeobright encounters the reddleman, Diggory Venn, who she has been told is looking for her. He informs her that he has her niece in his van, and Mrs. Yeobright immediately goes to the girl. She very soon learns from Thomasin that the girl has returned home alone from Anglebury, where she and Wildeve were to have been married earlier in the day, and that she is not yet married. Her aunt takes her in immediately to confront Wildeve and is not entirely satisfied with his explanation of what happened. In private conversation apart from Mrs. Yeobright, Wildeve answers Thomasin's questions by saying that, of course, he will still marry her.

Their discussion is interrupted by the arrival of the group from Rainbarrow, led by Fairway and Grandfer Cantle, who have come to serenade the supposed newlyweds. Wildeve is annoyed by their appearance but must put up with their congratulations and rambling conversation. By the time they leave he discovers Mrs. Yeobright and Thomasin have already gone, and he starts off toward Mistover Knap, assuming that the fire still burning in front of Captain Vye's is a signal from Eustacia.

Commentary

Whatever else might be said about the character of Diggory Venn, certainly Hardy uses him as a "connector" in the development of the plot (to employ a term from the English critic E. M. Forster). He is a natural for the part: his occupation as a reddleman makes him a characteristic part of the setting but yet a person who is always traveling and not really one of the heath folk; the kind of person he is gives him the necessary resourcefulness. A connector is a character who, though not important in himself to the main events of the story, brings about or makes possible these events. It is true that Venn eventually marries Thomasin Yeobright, in the Book Sixth that Hardy added to satisfy his readers. But he is in the novel primarily to do what he does in these chapters: he is the one who brings Thomasin back to her aunt. He is invariably in the right place at the right time to lend aid, offer advice in his humble way, or listen sympathetically to another with problems. His activity extends from bandaging Johnny Nunsuch's hand on one occasion to rescuing Clym Yeobright from death in the stream adjoining Shadwater Weir.

As has already been mentioned, Hardy makes light of the credulity of the heath folk, though he shows them as no more limited than any human being. He does so here, as many times elsewhere, in the long-winded discussion of the reputed musical ability of Thomasin's now dead father. But this in turn leads up to another variety of Hardy's humor, as shown in this sentence: "As with Farinelli's singing before the princesses, Sheridan's renowned Begum Speech, and other such examples, the fortunate condition of its being for ever lost to the world invested the deceased Mr. Yeobright's *tour de force* on that memorable afternoon with a cumulative glory which comparative criticism, had that been possible, might considerably have shorn down." In its apparently ponderous, certainly slow-breaking effect, this sentence is very much like something by Mark Twain. It is, of course, a variety of verbal humor.

CHAPTERS 6-7

Summary

On Rainbarrow again Eustacia Vye impatiently waits for Wildeve to heed her signal. After watching the inn for some time, she returns to the fire before her grandfather's house and persuades Johnny Nunsuch, her young assistant, to continue his work of feeding the blaze. When Wildeve signals his approach, she sends Johnny home and awaits Wildeve's appearance. Though she is pleased that she has made him come, in their conversation she is unable to get him to say he loves her more than he does Thomasin. Though they have been lovers in the past, each is now suspicious of the other's intentions. They part without any definite commitment to each other.

At some length Eustacia is described as more like a goddess than a woman.

Commentary

It is revealing to analyze the way Hardy develops a scene, and the one between Eustacia and Wildeve in these chapters is useful for discussion. The purpose of the scene, to show the reactions of old lovers who meet again, is made clear from the very beginning. When Wildeve appears, Eustacia laughs and is said to be full of "triumphant pleasure." Hardy writes of her: "She let her joyous eyes rest upon him without speaking, as upon some wondrous thing she had created out of chaos." As almost his first words, Wildeve is made to say: "You give me no peace. Why do you not leave me alone?" His reply undermines her feelings immediately, and the meeting is off on the wrong foot.

Not only does Wildeve not appear in the image Eustacia wants to have of him, but he makes her take the initiative in trying to define the relationship between them. Hardy makes her the stronger of the two personalities, a fact which Wildeve himself tacitly admits. It is she who brings up the subject of his marriage, who guesses at his motives for not yet going through with it, who compares herself with Thomasin. Wildeve, meanwhile, remains simply the critic, mildly complaining about what he calls his "curse of inflammability." Beyond words, even the gesture of showing him her face will not make him what Eustacia wants him to be.

Finally, Eustacia is made to ask for his love, but Wildeve will not commit himself. Thereafter, they take small vengeance on each other, ending in her refusal to let him touch her. The meeting has been one of conflicting intentions, skillfully shown in Wildeve's being said to bow his way out of the scene like "a dancing-master" and Hardy's comment on Eustacia: "She knew that he trifled with her; but she loved on." He uses her; she, him. It has always been so, it is clear, and always will be. What is said about Eustacia in the next chapter makes obvious that it will take more of a man than Wildeve to handle her or perhaps no man at all can.

"Eustacia Vye was the raw material of a divinity." Thus begins one of the famous passages in literature. But Hardy has prepared for it by hinting at mysteries in her character: her appearances on Rainbarrow, the reputation she has among the heath folk, her effect on Johnny Nunsuch, and the like. His description of her in chapter 7 is the most extensive static characterization in the novel, rivaled only by the space given Egdon Heath in the first chapter. What Hardy says about her is accurately summarized in the first sentence: she lookes different from other women on the heath, she has different reasons for living there, her desires are unlike those of others, and her interests and her habits set her apart. Indeed she is "raw material of a divinity."

Her differences from others are shown not simply by what Hardy says but by the imagery and allusions in which he embodies his comments. He remarks of her hair "that a whole winter [does] not contain darkness enough to form its shadow: it [closes] over her forehead like nightfall extinguishing the western glow." She has "Pagan eyes," and "the lines of her lips" are so fine "that, though full, each corner of her mouth [is] as clearly cut as the point of a spear." And he says that "her motions" recall "the ebb and flow of the sea." In short, the imagery he uses for Eustacia is very different from that he uses for other characters and for scenes and places; the latter imagery is full of analogies with terms peculiar to the locality (see the section on Style in Critical Analysis).

In describing her, Hardy also uses allusions, for example, to Mount Olympus, the Fates, the Sphinx, Hades, Alcinous, Phaeacia; to William the Conqueror, Napoleon, Saul, Pontius Pilate, Heloise, Cleopatra; to "bourbon roses, rubies, and tropical midnights." He searches through mythology and history to find equivalents for that "raw material" that makes Eustacia larger than life. Everywhere in the novel his range of allusion is wide, but it is particularly so for this character.

A young woman of "some forwardness of mind," Eustacia, like Clym, is capable of thinking beyond the usual concerns of the heath dwellers. She will be shown to complain about her lot in life, believing that she is cut out for great actions and great emotions. Here, she blames what she calls "Destiny" for not satisfying "her great desire," "to be loved to madness." Her complaint and the way in which her life is shown to turn out are embodiments of Hardy's theme in the novel.

She is quite capable of viewing her relationship to Wildeve with objectivity, though it does not stop her from at times trying to deceive herself. With an irony she herself recognizes, she knows that she idealizes Wildeve "for want of a better object." In the light of her eventual dissatisfaction with Clym, it is a real question as to whether she really knows what she wants.

Certainly her signaling of Wildeve is a romantic indulgence, the meaning of which she is half conscious of. It is a symbol reminiscent of others of a melodramatic nature used later in the book. Like Egdon Heath, Rainbarrow is the kind of symbol very typical of those in Hardy's fiction. Place has great meaning for the characters of his novels. The barrow is the setting for a great many important events and emotions. Eustacia is first viewed as she stands on its summit, at the end of her life she makes a final appearance there, in between she meets Wildeve at the top or nearby; even the last scene of the novel has Clym using it as his pulpit. But most of all it symbolizes the way Eustacia looks at life, both her strength and her weakness: from afar and apart from others.

CHAPTERS 8-9

Summary

His work for Eustacia completed, returning home Johnny Nunsuch is frightened by a strange light on the heath, returns to Captain Vye's to find Eustacia in conversation with Wildeve, and in perplexity goes back in the direction of the light. By chance his presence as he spies on what turns out to be the reddleman is discovered, and Venn quizzes the young boy. Johnny is afraid of Venn because he is a reddleman but reveals that Eustacia and Wildeve are meeting. After the boy leaves, Venn rereads an old letter from Thomasin rejecting his earlier offer of marriage, a fact which has put him into the reddle trade.

After several tries, he does manage to overhear what Eustacia and Wildeve say at a meeting in a ditch around Rainbarrow. Eustacia again can't get Wildeve to commit himself to her, or even to Thomasin, and she delays answering his question about going to America with him. As a result of listening in on the conversation, Venn decides to call on Eustacia.

Commentary

The reddleman is as much a part of the setting of Hardy's story as the furze. Johnny Nunsuch's reaction to being in the presence of the reddleman shows dramatically what is presented by means of exposition at the beginning of chapter 9. The boy's fear of Venn is the result of the supersititions and folklore that have attached themselves to the figure of the reddleman. His red color, which he cannot avoid and which Hardy mentions frequently, makes him seem to the credulous heath folk almost an emissary of Satan. To the children, certainly this is so. Johnny even says that he might be less frightened if Venn were a gipsy rather than a reddleman.

Hardy's use of coincidence in his novel is well known and often criticized. Some critics have suggested that coincidence is so often to be found because Hardy uses it as a way of expressing his idea that chance governs man's life more than man wishes to admit. In any case, by chance Johnny encounters Venn and tells him of accidentally overhearing the conversation between Eustacia and Wildeve. Whether this sequence of events is believable or not, it is convenient for Hardy's development of the plot to have Venn know what is going on. He is, after all, the connector in the story. As a consequence of finding out about the relationship between Eustacia and Wildeve, Venn goes to Eustacia to try to persuade her to intercede with Wildeve in Thomasin's behalf, and proposes himself to Mrs. Yeobright as a suitor for Thomasin. In turn, Mrs. Yeobright uses a second suitor as a lever to try to convince Wildeve to commit himself about Thomasin, and this causes Wildeve to hurry to Eustacia to get her to make up her mind about going off with him. All this from Johnny's coming on Venn by chance.

CHAPTERS 10-11

Summary

Venn calls on Eustacia and, unable to persuade her to help Thomasin, reveals that he has overheard her and Wildeve. The more Venn tries to argue her out of her relationship with Wildeve, the more determined she is to maintain it. Defeated here, Venn offers himself to Mrs. Yeobright as a suitor for Thomasin, asserting that he has loved her longer than Wildeve; but Mrs. Yeobright rejects his offer.

Mrs. Yeobright, in turn, speaks to Wildeve of the fact that another suitor is interested in her niece. Refusing to be hurried into a commitment, Wildeve rushes off to call on Eustacia, wanting her to decide right away if she will accept his offer to go off with him. She will not do so, now wondering if she really wants a man that a woman who is her social inferior has rejected.

Eustacia learns from her grandfather that Clym Yeobright is coming home to Egdon Heath for Christmas.

Commentary

The structure of the novel might be indicated by the rise and fall of a curve describing expectation. This curve traces the relationship between Clym Yeobright and Eustacia Vye and their aspirations (a relationship mirrored in that between Wildeve and Thomasin). In Book First the curve is rising, as shown in Eustacia's dissatisfaction with Wildeve and her longing for a man to satisfy her need for love and in Thomasin's provincial, limited desire to be satisfied with Wildeve because he is good enough for her and because her aunt wants no stain on her character. The rise is shown further, in a sense, in Wildeve's keeping himself in a position possibly to attract either Eustacia or Thomasin. Clym, of course, has not yet appeared.

Irony is everywhere in this novel, as would be expected in a story of tragic outcome. At least one instance has been singled out for comment. In these chapters, surely Venn's diligent efforts to help Thomasin are ironic, though he himself is unaware of it: his efforts only make Wildeve the more anxious to persuade Eustacia to go off with him. As many critics have remarked, irony is part of Hardy's characteristic view of the world.

Everything about a novel expresses its theme, from its structure to its briefest figure of speech. Nowhere is it expressed more overtly, however, than in its structure. The expectation and defeat which man's life gives evidence of reveal that he lives in a universe that is at least indifferent to him. That it may also be hostile is a suggestion that Hardy allows to lie undeveloped, for the most part, beneath everything he says.

BOOK SECOND

CHAPTERS 1-3

Summary

Eustacia overhears her grandfather and Humphrey and Sam discussing the kind of life Clym Yeobright has been living in Paris. Humphrey suggests, when Captain Vye leaves, that Eustacia and Clym would make a fine couple. The conversation sets her to daydreaming about Clym, and she walks down to look at the Yeobright house.

Meanwhile, Mrs. Yeobright and Thomasin are preparing for Clym's arrival: getting apples from the loft of the fuel house and gathering holly on the heath. Thomasin refuses to answer Mrs. Yeobright's question as to whether she still loves Wildeve and makes the older woman promise not to tell Clym of her troubles.

On the night Clym is to arrive, Eustacia waits on the heath for a glimpse of him as he goes by. When he does, with Mrs. Yeobright and Thomasin, Eustacia is unable to see him but can hear his voice. This causes her to dream an unusual dream about him. For the next few days she goes out in the hope of meeting him but does not.

Commentary

As early as chapter 3 of Book First Clym's coming home for Christmas has been mentioned. Eustacia is made to hear this news rather late and shows little reaction to it, since he left before she came to Mistover Knap. Several times in the first book, however, she is said to long for a man who, unlike Wildeve, is really equal to her. In these chapters, foreshadowing of Clym's coming and his effect on Eustacia's life is frequently used. She is made to overhear a conversation about him, she thinks and dreams about him, she walks near his house, she waits to see him when he arrives; Thomasin and Mrs. Yeobright prepare to welcome him home. The movement of the plot is entirely in the direction of Clym.

That Eustacia is a romantic has been suggested earlier in the novel; her ambition is "to be loved to madness." Here, this side of her comes to the fore. The overheard conversation causes her to think that the soon-to-arrive Clym is "like a man coming from heaven." She can think about nothing else, and she goes to hover about outside his house. That he is coming from Paris, to her "the center and vortex of the fashionable world," is overwhelmingly exotic. Hearing Clym's voice as he passes is enough to provide Eustacia with a remarkable dream, in which a mysterious male figure appears to her in "silver armour." As Hardy puts it, she is "half in love with a vision." She has fixed in her mind a romantic image of what Clym means to her long before she actually meets him. And the way by which she does meet him in the next chapters, by taking the part of one of the young men in the traditional Christmas play, is but another instance of this same side of her character.

CHAPTERS 4-6

Summary

Taking advantage of the fact that the mummers are practicing the traditional Christmas play in her grandfather's fuel house, Eustacia arranges to take Charley's place on the night it is to be given at Mrs. Yeobright's party in order to encounter Clym. Wearing Charley's costume, she joins the mummers that night, and they go to perform. While they are waiting for the dancing to end, she is recognized by some of the boys. She performs her part in the play, a part she has chosen so as not to reveal that she is a girl and to enable her to study the guests when her turn is over.

She observes Clym at leisure, but when the mummers are asked to sit down to eat she is made uncomfortable. When she sees Clym talking to Thomasin, she realizes he may fall in love with his cousin again but can do nothing on the present occasion because she is both dressed and treated as a boy. When she hurries outside, Clym follows her, guessing she is a woman; they talk briefly and generally. On her way home she remembers she was to have met Wildeve that night but doesn't care that she has missed him.

Commentary

Just as elsewhere Hardy uses traditions or customs to fill in the setting, for instance, the Fifth of November bonfires earlier and at the end of the novel the maypole festivities, here he describes the traditional Christmas mumming while at the same time using it to advance his plot. He says of such customs: "A traditional pastime is to be distinguished from a mere revival in no more striking feature than in this, that while in the revival all is excitement and fervor, the survival is carried on with a stolidity and absence of stir which sets one to wondering why a thing that is done so perfunctorily should be kept up at all." And just as earlier he quoted verses from some of the ballads Grandfer Cantle typically sings, here he quotes lines from *Saint George* to give the flavor of this particular "traditional pastime."

Eustacia's first look at Clym Yeobright is also the reader's first. Hardy renders just his face, since it is said to be his most revealing feature. It is asserted that Clym's face is "really one of those faces which convey less the idea of so many years as its age than of so much experience as its store." Adding to this, Hardy goes on to say that "an inner strenuousness [is] preying upon an outer symmetry, and they [rate] his look as singular." That he should be this kind of man from a precocious childhood is no great surprise. It is interesting and typically human that common talk about him before he actually returns to Egdon makes him into a person the man himself in no way resembles. This first impression of Clym is of a man who finds it difficult to live with himself.

He is also not the man Eustacia has been dreaming about. Hardy's description of Clym here is brief by comparison with his description of Eustacia in chapter 7, Book First. It is different in tone and in imagery. In short, Hardy is bringing together into the most important relationship in the book a woman who is "the raw material of a divinity" and a man who is prey to "an inner strenuousness." The fact of the way they are presented in itself predicts much about what will happen to both. It is impossible in reading this static description of Clym not to think of that one earlier of Eustacia.

CHAPTERS 7-8

Summary

When Eustacia next encounters Venn, she finds out that he is not really going to marry Thomasin and agrees to encourage the young woman's marriage to Wildeve. Venn volunteers to deliver a letter for Eustacia to Wildeve on Rainbarrow that night, and after reading its contents Wildeve is determined to marry Thomasin to make Eustacia suffer. Encouraged by Eustacia's remark, Venn calls on Thomasin to ask her to marry him, but Wildeve has got there first and already has her promise.

Thomasin is resolute in her decision to marry Wildeve, partly because of a letter from Clym, away visiting friends, who is shocked by hearing rumors of scandal in the relationship between his cousin and the innkeeper. Thomasin does not want Mrs. Yeobright to give her away, and she prefers the marriage to be over and done with before Clym returns. On the day of her wedding, shortly after she has gone off to meet Wildeve at the church, Clym returns home. Upon hearing an account of the abortive earlier attempt at marriage, Clym is annoyed at his mother for withholding news of Thomasin's affairs. Though he finally decides to walk to the church, before he can Venn arrives with a report of the wedding.

He tells them that Thomasin and Wildeve are indeed married and that Eustacia gave her away; however, he does not tell them that the latter was there at his request.

Commentary

As in the case of the marriages of Eustacia to Clym and Thomasin to Venn later in the novel, Hardy has here described the occasion of the marriage of Thomasin to Wildeve by report, not directly or dramatically. His reason for handling this important event in such a manner is to allow the character Venn to describe the wedding to those most vitally interested in it, Clym and Mrs. Yeobright. The reddleman, of course, is again acting in his role of connector. Immediately, he has caused Eustacia to be present at the ceremony. Hardy may also have handled the marriage as he does to emphasize the reasons for it and the consequences of it rather than the formal or social ceremony itself.

Certainly the occasion of the ceremony is full of irony, as are many other scenes in the novel. That Thomasin and Wildeve should be married in the presence only of Eustacia and Venn is part of the irony. Another is that Eustacia should be giving Thomasin away

The former is obviously "giving" Thomasin to Wildeve, since his attraction as an object of her desire "to be loved to madness" has been dimmed by the appearance of Clym.

If structure is thought of as indicated by a curve describing the rise and fall of expectation, Book Second shows the curve still on the rise. Clym appears on Egdon Heath, presumably on vacation from a reputedly successful career as manager for a diamond firm in Paris. To Eustacia he represents more of a man than Wildeve, someone who is equal to her view of life and her ambitions. She disposes of her earlier lover by his marriage to Thomasin. For Thomasin this marriage is a seal of respectability which will please her aunt and the community. For Wildeve it is mixed blessing, with the bitter taste of revenge against Eustacia for turning him away.

These events and relationships, to which structure gives shape, once again illustrate that somber theme of the novel discussed earlier. The certainty of failure is to be seen lurking in the questionable motives of Thomasin and Wildeve in marrying and in the romantic image of Clym quickly taking shape in Eustacia's mind. The curve is rising; but it will also fall.

BOOK THIRD

CHAPTERS 1-2

Summary

Clym is looked upon by the heath dwellers as a rather special person not only because of his unusual reputation as a boy but also because of his position in the diamond business in far-off Paris. Therefore, when he tells the group at the haircutting at Fairway's that he has come home to make himself into a schoolteacher they do not believe him. Mrs. Yeobright does not believe him either, but in her case it is because she does not want to. The conversation between them in which he tries to explain why he is giving up his job is interrupted by Christian Cantle. He relates the tale of Eustacia's being pricked in the arm with a stocking needle by Susan Nunsuch, a revenge the latter has planned because she is convinced that Captain Vye's granddaughter has bewitched her children.

Later, Clym questions Sam about Eustacia, wondering if she is the young woman who was disguised as a mummer at this mother's party. Sam suggests he can see Eustacia by coming to join several of the men in trying to retrieve the bucket from Captain Vye's well.

Commentary

It is appropriate that it should be Christian who reports the incident in church. He is the perfect barometer of the heath folk's superstitions. Earlier in the novel, he has been troubled by a discussion of ghosts and especially by the report of the appearance of a red ghost. He describes Susan's attack on Eustacia as if he believes witchcraft is a real concern.

Hardy makes particularly effective use of the "chorus" of villagers at the haircutting outside Fairway's house. To them Clym first reveals his plan for remaining on Egdon Heath to become "a schoolmaster to the poor and ignorant." Though he is said to be a "product" of the heath, his aspirations are beyond their understanding, and his values are not theirs. Hardy says of him "that in striving at high thinking he still [cleaves] to plain living," an aspect of him that they are unable to square with his career in Paris in the diamond trade. The haircutting scene humorously reveals the inability of the heath people to understand or even to take seriously the plan Clym describes. They take in the wrong way all of his remarks about his life in Paris and cannot make out why such a conspicuous success as Clym should want to return to the heath to do anything.

Mrs. Yeobright's repeated concern over the possible "stain" on Thomasin's character because of the mishap in her first attempt to marry Wildeve reveals much about the kind of woman Clym's mother is. Community opinion is important to her, though she is looked upon by others and herself acts as an "aristocrat" of the area. She is also inflexible in her view of life and in distinguishing right from wrong. It is not surprising, then, that she should be unable either to understand or to approve of her son's idea of becoming a schoolteacher. She goes so far as to say that he is something less than a man for not evincing ordinary ambition. She is intelligent enough, but her mind is restricted to a narrow view. She is a good deal less pliable in what she can accept than even the heath dwellers.

She is the kind of mother who lives too much through her own child's life. A sharp difference of opinion between her and her son over his career and other matters seems inevitable.

CHAPTERS 3-4

Summary

Clym does go to Captain Vye's, ostensibly to help with the lost bucket, actually to meet Eustacia. He meets her, and after she suffers a slight injury assisting him in getting water from the well, he tries to get her to admit she is the young woman he met in mummer's costume at Mrs. Yeobright's party. She will not admit anything, and they disagree over what the heath means to them.

At home the next day Mrs. Yeobright expresses annoyance at Clym's meeting Eustacia. But he continues to do so for the next few weeks until he and his mother quarrel bitterly over both his new career and his interest in Eustacia. Mrs. Yeobright is sure that he would not persist in his desire to be a teacher had he not met Eustacia.

The next evening Clym meets Eustacia on Rainbarrow, the signal for their tryst being the start of an eclipse of the moon. Urged on by his mother's criticism of Eustacia, he wants to marry the girl, but Eustacia will not commit herself, preferring that he tell her of Paris. Finally, she does agree to marry him, thinking he will soon forget his desire to be a schoolmaster and return to Paris.

Commentary

In the scene of the first meeting between Clym and Eustacia, Hardy makes the young woman the instigator of the encounter; however, since she has disguised herself as a mummer, she is not at first recognized as even a woman. When she is, she is in no position to reveal her identity, since her appearance may strike Clym as merely whimsical. But in the scene of the second meeting Clym is the instigator, though of course Eustacia makes sure she is available to meet him. She is more than willing to prolong the conversation with him and puts up with an injury to her hand with very little complaint. She shows her interest in him, in part, by frankly expressing her opinion of Egdon Heath, perhaps thinking he will share it or at least challenging him in her comment.

The scene in which Eustacia finally agrees to marry Clym occurs on Rainbarrow and is lighted by a moon that slowly moves into an eclipse. The symbolism of Rainbarrow has already been mentioned, and certainly Clym's meeting Eustacia here, as Wildeve has before, is a sign of his moving into her orbit. If Rainbarrow symbolizes her view of life, Egdon Heath might be said to symbolize Clym's. It might be added that Paris appears here and elsewhere as an ambiguous symbol: it represents all that is lively and worth living for to Eustacia and all that is idle and valueless to Clym.

Particularly interesting is Hardy's use of the moon as a symbol. When Eustacia makes her appearance on Rainbarrow the moon begins to go into eclipse; by the time she has promised to marry Clym and they part the eclipse is almost full. The significance for both their lives is plain enough. When Clym observes the moon before the eclipse and Eustacia's arrival, he sees it as perhaps "some world where personal ambition [is] not the only recognized form of progress" and imagines himself exploring its solitary wildness. Eustacia, after agreeing to marry Clym, reads into it her own meaning: "Clym, the eclipsed moonlight shines upon your face with a strange foreign color, and shows its shape as if it were cut out in gold. That means that you should be doing better things than this." Both readings are idealistic and romantic but represent conflicting images of Clym.

These conflicting ideas of what Clym should be produce one of the large ironies of the novel, clearly shown here. Eustacia wants Clym as the avenue to a glamorous life; Clym has returned to Egdon Heath to live a life of service. She promises to be his "for ever and ever," but is sure he "will never adhere to [his] education plan" and will eventually take her to Paris. He asks her to marry him, but thinks of her as a helpmate in his desire to be a "schoolmaster to the poor and ignorant." Clym is painfully conscious of the dilemma he now finds himself in: "Three antagonistic growths [have] to be kept alive: his mother's trust in him, his plan for becoming a teacher, and Eustacia's happiness." He is also somewhat, though not fully, aware of the irony of the cross-purposes in his relationship with Eustacia. Whatever her reasons, Mrs. Yeobright is in fact right in her assertion that Eustacia is the wrong woman for Clym. But as Hardy implies, all human beings, like Clym, pay little attention to what is right in fact. Or perhaps Hardy means to say men are fated to be wrongheaded.

CHAPTERS 5-6

Summary

When Mrs. Yeobright discovers that Clym and Eustacia are engaged, her comments to him are bitter and typical of those of a mother to a son. Clym tells his mother that he will move out of the house, and when he meets Eustacia he says they must marry right away, though it will mean living in a small cottage on the heath for a few months before he is ready to set up as a schoolteacher in Budmouth. He finds a cottage to rent, so that he can have some place to live even before they marry, and moves from his mother's house.

After Clym's departure, Mrs. Yeobright is visited by Thomasin, who is unable to console her. When Wildeve hears of Eustacia's approaching marriage, he immediately wants her again.

Commentary

Hardy says of Thomasin:

In her movements, in her gaze, she reminded the beholder of the feathered creatures who lived around her home. All similes and allegories concerning her began and ended with birds. There was as much variety in her motions as in their flight. When she was musing she was a kestrel, which hangs in the air by an invisible motion of its wings. When she was in a high wind her light body was blown against trees and banks like a heron's. When she was frightened she darted noiselessly like a kingfisher. When she was serene she skimmed like a swallow....

This constitutes a kind of essay on style by the author and is rather unusual in a work of fiction. Elsewhere, Hardy's imagery is full of analogy to local features and nature (see the section on Style in Critical Analysis).

Another series of incidents in these chapters is reminiscent of the consequences of Johnny Nunsuch's coincidental meeting with Venn in Book First. Mrs. Yeobright finally says to Clym, after they have quarreled again about his interest in Eustacia: "I wish that you would bestow your presence where you bestow your love!" As a result of the antagonism between mother and son, several things happen: Clym tells his mother he will move out of the house; he tells Eustacia they must marry at once and can live in a small cottage on the heath; he promises her they will have to live under such conditions only six months "if no misfortune happens"; Clym rents a cottage and moves out of his mother's house even before he marries Eustacia; Mrs. Yeobright is in despair when he does so and cannot be consoled by Thomasin; when he hears the news of the marriage Wildeve's interest in Eustacia quickly reawakens. All of this happens as the result of a quarrel. As in the case of the incidents mentioned in Book First, chance or perhaps even a more than indifferent governing power in the universe seems, according to Hardy, to disturb the lives of the characters. What is illustrated here, of course, is the theme of the novel.

CHAPTERS 7-8

Summary

While the marriage of Clym and Eustacia takes place, Mrs. Yeobright stays at home, miserable and unable to avoid thinking about it. When Wildeve calls to pick up something Thomasin was going to get from her aunt, though he doesn't know it is money, Mrs. Yeobright refuses to send the guineas with him but decides it would be a good time to send them to Thomasin and Clym, both of whom are at Mistover. She entrusts Christian Cantle with their delivery.

Christian falls in with a group going to a raffle at the Quiet Woman Inn and after, to his surprise winning it, he walks with Wildeve toward Mistover Knap to deliver the money. On the way when they pause for a rest, Christian is so fascinated by a pair of dice, with which he won the raffle and which Wildeve then gave him, that he wants to gamble with the innkeeper. When Wildeve discovers that Christian is carrying money for Thomasin, the innkeeper decides to win it all, at first to get back at Mrs. Yeobright, but later to benefit himself personally. Only after he has won all the money does Wildeve discover half of its is Clym's.

Having watched the game from the shadows, Venn appears and challenges Wildeve to continue. The reddleman succeeds in winning back all the money from Wildeve, though they must finish the game with light from glowworms and only one die. Not realizing that half of the money is Clym's, Venn stops Thomasin on her way home from the wedding celebration and gives her the 100 guineas.

Commentary

The raffle at the inn is, of course, an annual local event staged by a "packman" or peddler. Christian, the epitome of superstition among the heath folk, wins the "gown-piece," though as he says earlier no woman will have him. At first, he thinks the event is the devil's own work; but having won, Christian is fascinated by the power of the dice, so fascinated that he thinks he is lucky. He is then willing to forget his fears and gamble with Wildeve later on. As elsewhere, Christian is shown to be not different from the other heath dwellers but only an exaggerated version of them.

The scene of the desperate gambling with Wildeve, Christian, and then Venn is an appropriate and powerful symbol in the novel. Several descriptions make its symbolic use clear. Of Christian and Wildeve, Hardy says: "Both men became so absorbed in the game that they took no heed of anything but the pigmy objects immediately beneath their eyes; the flat stone, the open lantern, the dice, and the few illuminated fern leaves which lay under the light, were the whole world to them." Later, Hardy says of Wildeve and Venn, using a rather commonplace analogy: "But neither of the men paid much attention to these things, their eyes being concentrated upon the little flat stone, which to them was an arena vast and important as a battlefield." Great stress is placed on the flat stone; that it is meant to symbolize the world man lives in is obvious. They play at dice, but what game they play and exactly what the stakes are they only half know.

Of man's world in relation to the universe Hardy says: "Amid the soft juicy vegetation of the hollow in which [Wildeve and Venn] sat, the motionless and the uninhabited solitude, intruded the chink of guineas, the rattle of dice, the exclamations of the reckless players." In short, the actions of men scarcely ruffle the surface of the great world around them. This idea is consonant with the several times Hardy shows Clym aware of his insignificance in the universe.

The symbolic scene is also packed with irony. Christian, who is trusted with the money in preference to Wildeve and who is literally fearful of his own shadow, is puffed up by his assumed prowess with the dice and loses all the money. Winning the money from Christian finally for selfish reasons, Wildeve then immediately loses it to Venn. And Venn, so careful of Thomasin's welfare and risking his own money to get what is hers back, unwittingly gives all the guineas to Thomasin and as a result causes trouble instead of preventing it. Irony piles up on irony in this novel, as is appropriate.

The symbolism of gambling and the many ironies that arise in the scene illustrate the theme of the novel, as its many other aspects do. Certainly this is true of the structure. The curve of expectation is still on the rise here, with the marriage and Clym's confidence and enthusiasm about his plans for a new career. But there is some contrary movement: Mrs. Yeobright's opposition to Eustacia; the mix-up with the guineas. The time is approaching when the curve will begin to descend.

BOOK FOURTH

CHAPTERS 1-2

Summary

Clym and Eustacia live a secluded life in the house at Alderworth, and he resumes his study, though she still hopes he will eventually take her to Paris. Mrs. Yeobright, puzzled because Clym has never acknowledged receipt of the guineas and then learning from Christian that Wildeve won them in gambling, visits Eustacia while she is at Mistover Knap. Eustacia misunderstands the older woman's questions, and they quarrel bitterly. When Eustacia tells Clym of the occasion, she brings up Paris again.

Quite unexpectedly Clym experiences severe eye trouble, an "acute inflammation" caused by too many hours of reading, and is told that it may be months before it clears up. Eustacia is greatly depressed, but Clym decides to take up furze cutting with Hymphrey. On an occasion when Eustacia discovers Clym singing while he works, they have a conversation that is bitter under the surface, both seeming to admit they no longer feel about each other as they once did.

Commentary

Just as the gambling scene is a dramatic symbol, so also is Clym's loss of eyesight. Just as the world for the determined gamblers is reduced to the size of the flat stone, so Clym's world is now literally limited. "His daily life was of a curious microscopic sort, his whole world being limited to a circuit of a few feet from his person." Clym, who has come home from the great world of Paris to the smaller world of Egdon Heath, finds himself in an even smaller one. Yet, his aim in coming home has been to discover what is for him the greater world of service. It is well to remember, of course, that though Clym's injured eyesight is a symbol it is also a fact. This is an illustration of the way in which any novel or any work of art operates on more than one level simultaneously. So also is the gambling scene a fact or Rainbarrow or the moon or the heath.

The consequences of Venn's mistake about the 100 guineas are seen to begin in these chapters. Thinking that Wildeve has the money, Mrs. Yeobright takes the wrong approach with Eustacia, and a sharp quarrel ensues. Before this encounter Eustacia intended, at Clym's urging, to call on Mrs. Yeobright in the attempt to establish some sort of relationship with her. Because of the quarrel Eustacia, in turn, brings up the subject of Paris, a hope she has never let die, though she admits Clym has made no promise to take her there. This hope will always stand between her and her husband. Later, it is wishful thinking about the realization of this hope that leads her to consider Wildeve's offer to help her escape the heath.

CHAPTERS 3-4

Summary

Determined to fight off her depression, Eustacia decides to go to a "gipsying," or dance, in East Egdon. She is envious of the young people dancing, and later, surprised by Wildeve's presence there, she consents to dance with her former lover and enjoys it more than she can understand. Allowing Wildeve to walk part way home with her, she encounters Clym and Venn, though Wildeve leaves her before her husband can see him.

Sure he has seen Wildeve with Eustacia, Venn hurries to the inn and ascertains, from questioning Thomasin indirectly, that it was her husband. Thereupon, Venn keeps watch on Clym's house and on several occasions frustrates Wildeve's loitering outside the house and trying to communicate with Eustacia. Venn also calls on Mrs. Ycobright, urging her to establish relations with both Clym and Thomasin for the good of all. She decides to forgive Clym and call on him. At the same time Clym tells Eustacia he must do something to improve relations with his mother.

Commentary

The gipsying at East Egdon Eustacia attends is another characteristic part of the setting of the heath. Hardy presents it as a self-contained experience set apart from ordinary life: "A whole village-full of sensuous emotion, scattered abroad all the year long, surged here in a focus for an hour. The forty hearts of those waving couples were beating as they had not done since, twelve months before, they had come together in similar jollity. For the time Paganism was revived in their hearts, the pride of life was all in all, and they adored none other than themselves." A footnote to this description is the repeated comments, by Hardy and through his characters, about the indifference to churchgoing on the part of the heath dwellers.

In her present frame of mind, annoyed with Clym and longing for Paris, Eustacia fits easily into this atmosphere with Wildeve, so easily that it frightens her. She experiences, like the others, the feelings Hardy described in the quotation given above.

As elsewhere, Hardy here foreshadows an important event to come in the story: Eustacia's suicide. Eustacia is thinking of her situation with Clym in the little cottage on the heath: "To Eustacia the situation seemed such a mockery of her hopes that death appeared the only door of relief if the satire of Heaven should go much further." She is getting desperate, though she has been married only a short time. Her view of what she ought to be doing comes into sharper and sharper focus even as the chance for realizing it quickly recedes. Eustacia decides she'll be "bitterly merry, and ironically gay" and will "laugh in derision." She then goes to the gipsying.

CHAPTERS 5-6

Summary

On an extremely hot day at the end of August Mrs. Yeobright sets off across the heath to call on Clym and Eustacia. Losing her way to the unfamiliar Alderworth, she is told to follow a furze cutter going along a path. She does so, only to realize finally that it is her son Clym. Resting in a clump of trees near Clym's house, she sees a man come to the house before she can get there.

It is Wildeve, come to call on Eustacia in the daytime. She admits him, and they talk in a room where Clym is asleep on the hearth rug. They discuss her marriage, Wildeve hinting that he is still in love with her. When Mrs. Yeobright knocks on the front door, Eustacia doesn't know what to do, finally deciding that Clym will probably awaken and answer the door. She quickly lets Wildeve out the back. When she returns, she finds Clym still asleep and Mrs. Yeobright no longer at the door.

Mrs. Yeobright has already started for home, previously overheated and exhausted and now shocked because Clym has apparently allowed Eustacia to refuse her entrance. The older woman encounters Johnny Nunsuch, who goes a short distance with her and is upset by her appearance. When he leaves her, she finally sits down to rest, watching a heron flying gracefully in the sky.

Commentary

Hardy makes the oppressive heat of the late August day a tangible factor in Mrs. Yeobright's journey of reconciliation to her son's house. He shows how it affects the plant and animal life that she encounters on the way. It takes its toll of the older woman, literally slowing her pace and placing a great strain on her constitution. Hardy demonstrates this effectively through the eyes of Johnny Nunsuch, with his comments about her "white and wet" face, her head "hanging-down-like," her movements like the "jerk and limp of an invalid," and her breathing like that of "a lamb when you drive him till he's nearly done for." The heat is virtually a character in these chapters, even almost a symbol.

Wildeve's arrival just before Mrs. Yeobright is ready to appear at her son's house after an exhausting walk is a coincidence like many others in the novel. It is convenient for Hardy to have some excuse available for Eustacia so that she doesn't admit Mrs. Yeobright but is not clearly at fault. On the other hand, as suggested before, Wildeve's appearance may be meant to suggest the operation of chance, or something more malign, in human life.

The scene between Eustacia and Wildeve here makes an instructive comparison with that between the same two characters in Book First, chapters 6-7. In both scenes Eustacia and Wildeve are meeting after a long separation; however, the second scene occurs after Eustacia's marriage. In the first, Eustacia is trying to make Wildeve measure up to the image she wants to have of him, knowing all along she doesn't really desire him. Here, Hardy reveals her acutely aware of the disadvantage to which Clym shows simply by physical description of the two men: beside the sleeping Clym are his "leggings, thick boots, leather gloves, and sleeve-waistcoat"; Wildeve is "elegantly dressed in a new summer suit and light hat." At a superficial glance, Wildeve appears to Eustacia more nearly to satisfy her desire in life: "what is called life — music, poetry, passion, war, and all the beating and pulsing that is going on in the great arteries of the world." No amount of rationalization of what Clym is, not even calling him a St. Paul, assuages Eustacia's sharp sense of having lost out by marrying him. In fact, neither Clym nor Wildeve is what she wants.

Johnny Nunsuch is a very believable child. He tags along after Mrs. Yeobright by instinct, as Hardy says. He is a keen observer of her condition, and is both frightened and awed by the condition she is in. He doesn't know what to do: he'd like to help but he wants to get home. With but a few details Hardy has the boy complete. He is an important character later when he repeats a remark Mrs. Yeobright makes to him on this occasion to Clym, in the scene in which the older woman dies. The sure touch with which Hardy presents this character is typical of the way he handles most of the minor characters in the novel.

For a set piece to illustrate Hardy's narrative style at its best, nothing serves better than the description of the heron Mrs. Yeobright

watches in flight at the end of chapter 6. It is not a purple passage
not overwritten; the language is controlled and the imagery appropriate. Furthermore, it serves admirably to help express Mrs.
Yeobright's feelings at this point in the story.

CHAPTERS 7-8

Summary

Though Eustacia objects, fearful that he will find out what she
has done, Clym is determined to waste no more time in going to see
his mother. On the way he discovers her prostrate and carries her to
a hut not far from Blooms-End. When he returns with help, they
discover she has been bitten by an adder, and they decide that until
a doctor can be brought the only thing to do is to use the old
remedy of treating her with the fat of another adder.

Meanwhile, Eustacia, waiting impatiently at home, starts out to
meet Clym but is halted momentarily by the arrival of Captain Vye,
with news that Wildeve has inherited eleven thousand pounds.
Thinking of Wildeve in a new light, Eustacia starts for Blooms-End,
only to meet the man who occupies her thoughts. After Wildeve
describes what he plans to do with the money and they are about
to part, they come upon the group at the hut. They conceal themselves behind the hut and learn that Mrs. Yeobright is dying. Both
Clym and Thomasin are there, with the heath folk, and after Mrs.
Yeobright dies Johnny Nunsuch repeats the remark about Clym that
his mother made earlier in the child's presence.

Commentary

It is useful to remember that each book in the novel ends with
a dramatic event partly as the result of the necessity Hardy felt to
satisfy the demands of serial publication. The reader must be kept
interested from month to month, and this was but one way to do so.

The scene of Mrs. Yeobright's death, the dramatic incident with
which this book ends, is full of irony: she is surrounded by those
people who have unwittingly made possible the conditions for her
being bitten by the adder. Clym has delayed in carrying out his
desire to reconcile with his mother as soon as possible; Eustacia

does not open the door to her, thinking that Clym will surely wake up and do so; Wildeve appears at Clym's house at the wrong moment and causes Eustacia to hesitate over whether or not to admit Mrs. Yeobright. All of them have reasons for what they do; yet, the woman lies dead.

This as well as the now falling curve by which the structure of the novel is described (falling because, for instance, Clym's eyesight fails, Clym and Eustacia begin to feel alienated from each other, and Mrs. Yeobright dies) once more embodies the theme of the novel. This theme — to repeat, man living in an indifferent, if not hostile, universe — is also shown directly in other places in these chapters: in Eustacia's refusing to accept blame for not letting Mrs. Yeobright in but instead placing it upon "the shoulders of some indistinct, colossal Prince of the World, who [has] framed her situation and [rules] her lot"; in Wildeve's unexpected inheritance, a large sum of money to a man whose worth is at least questioned by almost all the characters in the story.

BOOK FIFTH

CHAPTER 1

Summary

For several weeks after his mother's death, Clym lies ill and sometimes irrational. He blames himself for her death and will not be consoled by Eustacia. Even Thomasin, for whom he once had a special affection, cannot comfort him. When Wildeve calls for his wife, Eustacia uses the opportunity to speak of her despair to her former lover, who advises her never to tell Clym that he was in the house when Mrs. Yeobright called.

Commentary

The chapter is used primarily as a summary one, in which Clym's grief of the past few weeks is epitomized. What he says to Eustacia and then Thomasin is but the latest repetition of what he has said all along. His attitude toward himself here is reminiscent of the self-pity he shows, for example, at the beginning of chapter 3 in the last book. By that time his forbearing attitude toward what has happened to him as the result of his eye trouble is beginning to wear thin. He almost taunts Eustacia about his reduced state of life. This is an unattractive, though humanly understandable, side of Clym in in his affliction.

That Clym's grief over his mother's death is so deep foreshadows the likelihood of great anger with Eustacia when he discovers she did not admit Mrs. Yeobright when she called on the memorable day. Even Eustacia repeats to Wildeve the proverb "Beware the fury of a patient man."

Certainly Clym's blaming himself for his mother's death is ironical: he doesn't know the conditions responsible for it; he is unaware, for example, that his mother did indeed call on him. Further, he doesn't realize that the remark repeated by Johnny Nunsuch, so crushing to him, was uttered by his mother in just such an extremity of mind as he himself is now in.

CHAPTERS 2-3

Summary

Having recovered from his illness, Clym questions Christian Cantle—who has come to announce the birth of Thomasin's child—about the day his mother died, and discovers she planned to visit her son's house. Christian tells him that Venn talked with Mrs. Yeobright that day, and Clym is anxious to find the reddleman. When Venn calls, not knowing Mrs. Yeobright is dead, Clym learns from him that she forgave her son; but Clym is puzzled by the discrepancy between this and the remark Johnny repeated. From Johnny he then learns that Mrs. Yeobright was coming from Alderworth when he fell in with her and that a man preceded her to the house and Eustacia looked out but did not admit her.

Clym immediately accuses Eustacia of cruelty to his mother and deception of himself with another man. Restraining himself from striking her, he rails at her until she can take no more, and she defends herself but without answering his questions. Then she leaves the house.

Shortly after, the servant tells Clym that Thomasin has decided to name her new baby Eustacia Clementine.

Commentary

Aroused by Christian's information, Clym sets out with determination to discover as much as he can about the day his mother died. His search necessarily leads him to Eustacia. This completes the irony begun in chapter 1: it is not he who is immediately responsible for Mrs. Yeobright's death; though no one in fact is, it is Eustacia's inadvertency that provides part of the conditions for it.

In almost every particular, the accusation scene between Clym and Eustacia is strongly reminiscent of a Shakespearean play, *Othello* perhaps. But Clym is a modern man, and unlike Othello does not put out his beloved's light; he exercises self-restraint. However, his rage is as towering as that of the Moor: they are men who cannot be betrayed. Even the gestures (Clym's seizing the sleeve of Eustacia's gown, his smashing the desk) and the language ("By my wretched soul you sting me, Eustacia! I can keep it up, and hotly too." "Do you brave me? do you stand me out, mistress?") strike the eye and ear as Shakespearean. Like Othello Clym also "kills" in ignorance of the truth. Eustacia, though a very different character from Desdemona, realizes that nothing she can say will stop Clym from expending his anger.

Clym's gesture of love, tying the strings of the bonnet Eustacia cannot manage, is both revealing and again reminiscent of the reluctance and gentleness with which the Moor dispatches his wife. The greatest love can turn quickly to the deepest hatred.

CHAPTERS 4-5

Summary

Knowing nowhere else to go, Eustacia returns to her grandfather's house. She is looked after by Charley, her admirer from the time before she was married. When she contemplates too long the pistols in Captain Vye's room, he removes them, later replying to her questions that he cannot allow her to injure herself.

Charley tries to amuse her in the days that go by but with little success. Since she has wanted a bonfire on the Fifth of November the previous two years, though he hasn't known the real reason for it, he builds one for her. When aware of its being lit, Eustacia first doesn't want it, then lets it burn, though she realizes it may bring Wildeve. It does, and he sympathizes with her, finally offering to help her in any way he can. She wants to get to Budmouth and then to Paris but agrees only to let Wildeve know if she will allow him to help and/or go with her.

Commentary

From this point on in Book Fifth the novel is, in a sense, all plot; that is, the time for speaking is past. Eustacia's hovering around the pistols in Captain Vye's bedroom the day she returns there is an even stronger foreshadowing of her eventual suicide than has occurred before. The stronger the foreshadowing of an event in a novel, the nearer it is to taking place.

The fact that Charley hides the pistols in the stable is not likely to stop Eustacia from destroying herself. The conversation with Wildeve is in somewhat the same spirit: in effect, they speak to each other in the past tense, though they are talking about the immediate future. It is too late for Wildeve to offer anything. Though he is shown not to realize this — he is, after all, an opportunist from first to last in the story — Eustacia does, though she goes through the motions of making plans with him.

The futility of her taking any action but that which is inevitable is shown in the fact that the story is back where it began, the Fifth of November. If anything, Eustacia has a worse opinion of herself than she did in the beginning: "her state was so hopeless that she could play with it." Hereafter, she moves without animation, Hardy showing her to be in the grip of the Destiny she has often referred to.

CHAPTER 6

Summary

Now living at his mother's house, Clym waits, expecting to hear from Eustacia. On the Fifth of November evening he goes to see Thomasin and Wildeve, though he doesn't know Wildeve is then on his way to see Eustacia at her grandfather's house. Since Thomasin doesn't know, he tells her of the state of affairs between himself and his wife, and his cousin advises him to contact Eustacia. When he gets home, he writes her a letter, inviting her to return.

When Wildeve returns home from Mistover Knap, Thomasin questions him closely enough about this walk and others to annoy him.

Commentary

As chapter 1 in this book is a summary one, this chapter is used for purposes of transition. Nothing really happens; everything is reaching dead center. Hardy shows, for instance, that Clym is delaying any contact with Eustacia as he did with his mother before the fateful journey across the heath. Obviously, some decisive action is imminent. Clym, Eustacia, Thomasin, Wildeve—all are faced in their personal destinies with questions and no answers.

CHAPTERS 7-8

Summary

Deciding on the next evening, the sixth, to leave, Eustacia signals Wildeve as planned. When the letter for her from Clym arrives, she is in her bedroom, and Captain Vye doesn't give it to her because he assumes she is asleep. When he finally realizes she has left the house it is too late. Though it is now raining, Eustacia determines to go ahead with her plans. She goes to the top of Rainbarrow, and thinking of what she is doing and how little it promises, she is in despair. Meanwhile, Susan Nunsuch, having seen Eustacia earlier in the evening about the time Johnny says he is feeling even more ill than he has been, makes an effigy of Eustacia in wax, sticks it with pins, and burns it in a fire.

Clym, hoping that Eustacia will come to him even though the night is stormy, is disappointed when Thomasin instead calls. She tells him she is sure Eustacia and Wildeve are going to run off together. Captain Vye also calls, recounting for Clym the story of Eustacia's thoughts of suicide with his pistols. After both men leave, Thomasin waits in Clym's house as long as she can, and then she starts off for the Quiet Woman Inn with her child. Losing her way, she comes upon Venn, who goes with her to guide her to her destination.

Commentary

The heath folk's superstitious beliefs are made overt in the scene in which Susan Nunsuch, long suspicious that Eustacia is a witch and is working evil on her son Johnny, makes an effigy of Eustacia in beeswax, pierces it many times with pins, and burns it in the fire. The Lord's Prayer said backward is an incantation which, as Hardy remarks, is "usual in proceedings for obtaining unhallowed assistance against an enemy." Sticking an image full of pins is common in voodoo, too.

Even as the image of Eustacia is melting in Susan's fire, so the young woman herself is "melting" on Rainbarrow, that symbolic projection which is the highest point on the heath. The barrow has meant much to Eustacia: from it she has viewed the heath, both nature and man. On it, in effect, she takes her last look at the world, even as at the end of the novel we see Clym practicing his newfound vocation on it. Eustacia just before death stands upon a monument to death. She looks at the world and sees nothing good: "I was capable of much; but I have been injured and blighted and crushed by things beyond my control!" She cannot return to Clym, she thinks, and Wildeve is not worthy of her. The foreshadowings of suicide earlier in the novel make clear what she will do.

So too is the storm on the heath symbolic; of Eustacia Hardy says: "Never was harmony more perfect than that between the chaos of her mind and the chaos of the world without." But not merely for her. The plot shows a confused pattern of people moving helter-skelter over the heath. With the storm comes the element of melodrama, to be climaxed by the deaths in the stream near the weir. The storm rages as it did in many nineteenth-century novels: significantly but unbelievably.

No one's presence is shown more at random during this night than Eustacia's. After her appearance on the barrow, she is never shown directly again until her body is glimpsed in the stream by Wildeve and pulled out by Venn. Her movements are known only by hint and report; Venn himself almost sees her on the heath. In these chapters, too, another of Hardy's coincidences occur: the business with the letter from Clym to Eustacia. By chance she never receives it.

Ironically, then, Eustacia goes off to Rainbarrow and her death without knowing that Clym has asked her to return, not whole-heartedly, to be sure, but he has asked. But even this is too late. Events rush to their conclusion in spite of what any character does, or at least this is what Hardy intends to show.

CHAPTER 9

Summary

Having left with a horse and gig, Wildeve waits below the inn for Eustacia's appearance. But it is Clym who approaches, looking for Eustacia, and just as he and Wildeve recognize each other, Clym hears what is clearly a body falling into the swollen stream adjoining Shadwater Weir. Both men, sure it is Eustacia who has fallen in or jumped, rush to her aid. Wildeve is less cautious, jumping in as soon as he sees her body; Clym goes to the rescue after trying to determine how best to go about it. Seeing what has happened, Venn, now approaching with Thomasin, sends her to the inn and effects the rescue of both men. With the help that arrives, he retrieves Eustacia's body. Only Clym survives.

Venn, in the inn, watches a servant dry the bank notes that were in Wildeve's pockets and must tell Charley, who calls on the Captain's behalf, that Eustacia is dead. Clym appears and takes both Venn and the young man upstairs to see the bodies of Eustacia and Wildeve. To Venn Clym blames himself for his wife's death.

Commentary

It is a year and a day since the first scene in the novel. As most critics have pointed out, Hardy observes the Aristotelian unity of time in this book, as well as the unity of place. It is, therefore, of some interest that the novel doesn't end here; there is still Book Sixth to come. As already mentioned (in Hardy's Life and Career; see also Commentary on Book Sixth), the final book is Hardy's concession to his readers.

If the storm on the heath is a melodramatic symbol, so also is the stream near the weir. In any literary work, water can be a symbol of either death or life, or even both. In nineteenth-century novels it was almost invariably a symbol of death. And water was frequently used as a means of suicide. Some critics have raised the question of whether Eustacia's death is in fact a suicide. The question seems hardly worth raising. Everything in the novel—specific foreshadowing, the tendency of events, the theme Hardy is demonstrating—points to suicide.

It is of course ironical that both Clym and Wildeve attempt to rescue Eustacia: her husband and her lover, from both of whom she is really estranged. Likewise ironical is the fact that neither is able to do so and must themselves be pulled out by the ever-present Venn, Hardy's connector in the plot. Clym insists he's the cause of his wife's death, as earlier he has broken down under the self-accusation about his mother's death. Unlike Eustacia Clym seems unaware of the notion that man is faced with an incomprehensible universe. In Book Sixth he overtly refuses, as Hardy says, to blame Destiny or God for his lot in life. Whatever Clym may think, his own life serves as one of the prime examples of what Hardy is trying to say in the book.

So, the fall of the curve of structure is now complete. First, Mrs. Yeobright; now, Eustacia and Wildeve. Clym is left with nothing, except perhaps the vestiges of his plans. Hardy has Venn sum up as he sits in the kitchen of the Quiet Woman Inn: "Two were corpses, one had barely escaped the jaws of death, another was sick and a widow." The heath remains as it was in the beginning: untouched, unmoved.

BOOK SIXTH

CHAPTERS 1-4

Summary

Though at Wildeve's death Thomasin receives a substantial inheritance, she moves in with Clym by choice. Clym occupies himself in preparing for his vocation of preacher. Venn calls, now a dairy farmer and normal in color, and Thomasin is pleased to see him. On Maypole Day Venn manages to obtain one of Thomasin's gloves, worn by her servant girl, though Thomasin herself does not go to the festivities.

After discovering from the servant what Venn has done, Thomasin encounters him while taking her daughter Eustacia for an airing: they see each other often after this meeting. Thinking he is obligated to do so because of his mother's wishes when she was alive, Clym is about to ask Thomasin to marry him when she tells him she wants to marry Venn. First disapproving because of his mother's memory, then approving, Clym offers no obstacle to Thomasin's marrying Venn.

On the day of the wedding the heath folk are helping Fairway stuff a mattress with feathers as a gift to the newlyweds. After giving the bride away, Clym wishes to have nothing to do with the wedding party and wanders off. He encounters Charley and gives him a lock of Eustacia's hair as a remembrance. After the party Venn and Thomasin go off to Venn's farm, leaving Clym alone in the house at Blooms-End.

Shortly thereafter, Clym begins practice of his vocation of wandering preacher, starting with an appearance on Rainbarrow.

Commentary

The fact that Hardy added this book to his original conception of the novel causes many consequences, most of which are obvious enough. For example, it blunts the effectiveness of his demonstration of the idea that man lives in an indifferent, perhaps hostile, universe. Hardy, in speaking of the fact that Clym, unlike Eustacia, does not blame either Destiny or God for his fate, says: "Human beings, in their generous endeavor to construct a hypothesis that shall not degrade a First Cause, have always hesitated to conceive a dominant power of lower moral quality than their own; and, even while they sit down and weep by the waters of Babylon, invent excuses for the oppression which prompts their tears." But indeed Eustacia Vye never hesitates to blame Destiny, which she always thinks of as having a questionable "moral quality." The whole movement of the first five books is unmistakably in this direction of questioning the power that governs the universe. In this novel Hardy depicts the universe as essentially indifferent to man rather than, as in later novels (notably *Jude the Obscure*), hostile to him.

The structure which embodies Hardy's theme is logically completed with the deaths of Wildeve and Eustacia at the end of Book Fifth. The defeat to Clym's emotional life and his planned career has already occurred. True, he becomes an "itinerant open-air preacher" in Book Sixth, but for the purposes of the structure of the novel this hardly matters. Obviously the unity of time represented by the year and a day during which the first five books take place is destroyed by the addition of events in the last book covering more than eighteen months. And if, as some critics have asserted, Hardy also achieves a unity of action in the novel (from signal fire to signal fire, as it were), then it too is disrupted by the additional book.

In Book Sixth Venn, whom Hardy uses previously as the connector in the plot, is made to change into the role of active suitor for Thomasin and does marry her. (Venn even literally changes color, from red to white.) The reason for this certainly must be to provide a happy ending for Thomasin, the gentle girl who asks little from life and gets less, at least in the first five books.

From the point of view of the critic or student of the novel, Hardy's addition of a final book is clearly an unfortunate mistake. His own justification for what he did has already been discussed (in Hardy's Life and Career). But to second-guess an author is futile; the reader must take, though not necessarily like, the work as it is delivered.

ANALYSES OF MAIN CHARACTERS

CLYM (CLEMENT) YEOBRIGHT

Clym, the native who returns to his birthplace on Egdon Heath, is an instance of a precocious, highly regarded child and boy who, when a man, leaves his provincial background to make his way in the world but who then gives up worldly success for what he thinks of as a more important calling on his native ground. In short, Hardy's protagonist is a character who, though still admired locally, is bound to be misunderstood when he chooses to forgo conventional ideas of vocation and success.

It might even be said that he anticipates a kind of martyr's role. Both the heath folk and his mother are doubtful of his plan to be a "schoolmaster to the poor and ignorant"; they view it as impractical as well as less desirable than his commercial career in Paris. Eustacia considers it incomprehensible that a man who has lived in Paris, the center, to her, of all that is gay and desirable, should choose to return to Egdon. His mother further objects to his desire to marry Eustacia, whom she considers an idle young woman. In short, from the very first Clym finds opposition to his plan. But he will persist; in fact, Hardy may be indicating that he is more persistent even as he is more strongly opposed.

At the basis of Clym's desire to serve his native Egdon lies a general and idealistic view of his fellow human beings: "Yeobright loved his kind. He had a conviction that the want of most men was knowledge of a sort which brings wisdom rather than affluence. He wished to raise the class at the expense of individuals rather than individuals at the expense of the class. What was more, he was ready at once to be the first unit sacrificed." At the end of the novel, his eyesight still subnormal, his mother and his wife dead, Clym still persists in the same view of mankind, will not complain of the injustice of his lot in life. Though his original plan is considerably reduced in scope, he mounts the summit of Rainbarrow in his role of "itinerant open-air preacher" with as much optimism, Hardy indicates, as he would have shown had his dream of a school actually come true.

As an individual, Clym is about as unsuited to be a husband as Eustacia is to be a wife. At one point, Eustacia describes him to Wildeve as a St. Paul and remarks that the qualities summed up in this allusion hardly make him a good companion. The phrase that describes him best is "inner strenuousness." He is as Spartan in his style of life as a Thoreau; at the least, this makes him hard to get along with, not merely for his wife, but for any other human being. It is ironical that in this aspect of his personality he is so much like his mother, who is inflexible in her attitude toward her son. Almost the only person in the novel with whom Clym is shown to be content is Humphrey, when the two of them cut furze together.

However admirable Clym's personality may be, certain sides of it are unattractive. That this should be so is a tribute to Hardy's ability to create lifelike characters. Clym is inclined to self-pity, and he has in him a curious unwillingness to act. His delay in trying to establish contact with his mother after his marriage is repeated in his hesitating to ask Eustacia to come back to him. His inability to act enables Hardy to show him at the mercy of events or circumstances or chance, a demonstration of the theme of the novel. He is meant to be, in other words, a modern man: able to understand but unable to act decisively.

EUSTACIA VYE

"Queen of night," Eustacia, who is a native of the fashionable seaside resort of Budmouth and whose non-English father gives her an appearance that is slightly exotic, is ever an outsider on Egdon Heath. Her grandfather's house is isolated physically, and she keeps herself apart from the heath dwellers by her walks alone and her frequent nightly excursions to the summit of Rainbarrow. She has a kind of contempt for the natives, as shown, for example, in her condescension to Charley in allowing him to hold her hand in payment for the part she wants to play in the Christmas mumming.

They, in turn, look upon her as unfriendly and too proud; Mrs. Yeobright tells Clym she is idle and probably wanton. Susan Nunsuch even thinks of her as a witch. Unlike Clym, whom the heath folk can at least fathom in part, Eustacia is beyond their comprehension. Only Charley has really had any opportunity to get to know her.

Her view of life is as foreign to the heath as her person: "in Eustacia's brain were juxtaposed the strangest assortment of ideas, from old time and from new. There was no middle distance in her perspective: romantic recollections of sunny afternoons on an esplanade, with military bands, officers, and gallants around, stood like gilded letters upon the dark tablet of surrounding Egdon." She is a hedonist for whom love as an end in itself is the greatest pleasure: "To be loved to madness—such was her great desire."

And she takes perverse pleasure in being unconventional in small ways. Hardy uses several phrases to describe her reaction to life, among the most striking of which is "smoldering rebelliousness."

Her whole personality has a slumberous, unawakened cast to it. The modern reader would no doubt say that Eustacia was either unaroused or as yet unsatisfied sexually. Certainly some of the descriptive details Hardy uses about her suggest this: for example the way in which she takes pleasure from having her hair caressed, either when brushed or when she accidentally walks under a bush and it touches her hair. When she says on one occasion to Wildeve that they were once "hot lovers," it is not clear that she means more than that they were emotionally involved. That she is difficult to be around or to live with is clear. Of this Hardy says: "She had the passions and instincts which make a model goddess, that is, those which make not quite a model woman." Though she is beautiful in an exotic way, she often acts very much like a spoiled child.

Vocal in her condemnation of Destiny, Eustacia is an active demonstration of Hardy's theme in the novel. Yet, there is something unattractive about her readiness to shift the blame for everything that happens to her; perhaps this is but another way in which she is not entirely English. It is difficult to accept whatever rationalization she makes for doing away with herself. It seems somehow unnecessary for a young woman of twenty to throw herself in a stream because she cannot find the ideal mate. Or maybe to say this is to admit to being a modern reader, who usually finds it difficult to believe in a romantic view of life.

It is a real question in the novel as to who is the main character. Hardy intended Clym to be, but Eustacia succeeds in upstaging him most of the time. Judged on the basis of the most widespread effects on the lives of the other characters in the novel, Eustacia clearly is more important. One way to see how this is possible is to imagine how Clym, Mrs. Yeobright, Thomasin, Wildeve, and Venn would have acted in the same setting had Eustacia been a different kind of person, a Thomasin, for instance. Clym himself affects others only insofar as he has a relationship to Eustacia. As with the addition of a sixth book to the original five, the reader has to take the novel as Hardy wrote it; and certainly he intended it to be a story about Clym Yeobright.

MRS. YEOBRIGHT

Clym's mother is "a well-known and respected widow of the neighborhood, of a standing which can only be expressed by the word genteel." The fact that "though her husband [was] a small farmer she herself [is] a curate's daughter" sets her apart from the heath folk and causes them to respect her presence. She is conventional in her views, looking upon material success, for instance, as a mark of a man's worth in life. Not being a woman of means, she is unable to understand how her son can give up his position in Paris and entertain such a foolish idea as that of teaching the poor on the heath. When Clym thinks of setting up a school in Budmouth, she immediately takes it as a sign of his coming to his senses.

Her repeated concern over the slight to Thomasin's character and that of her family from the young woman's delayed marriage to Wildeve says much about her as a person. Appearances and reputation are important to her; she is shocked, for example, by the sight of her son dressed as a furze cutter. She had thought it was only a diversion or hobby for him. Her relationships to Clym and her niece Thomasin are rather austere; she habitually reacts to them by giving advice. The very thing which has sustained her in her widowhood turns out finally to undo her: her inflexibility of judgment. Were it not for this, she would not have been on the heath at all on the fateful August day. Chance, perhaps, operates to bring Wildeve into Clym's house before her, and as a result she is overly exhausted by the time she starts home. Ironically, she is as hard on herself, often needlessly, as her son is on himself; the very way in which they are alike keeps them apart too long.

THOMASIN (TAMSIN) YEOBRIGHT

The gentle Thomasin is the young innocent who through no lack of goodwill and right intentions on her part is treated roughly by circumstances or, in Hardy's view, by the sort of world man lives in. She is so normal and conventional in her views and her personality that it is easy to forget that she takes any part in the story. She wants to do right by everybody, is equitably and kindly treated by everyone but her husband, and by the end of the novel is conveniently disposed of for a happy future. It is possible to say that Hardy added the sixth book solely to make things come out right for her; at least, his readers seemed to have demanded it. It is hard to question these readers' desire: no one likes to see the innocent mistreated.

Her only fault, from her aunt's point of view, is that she persists in wanting to marry Wildeve even after she has not been well treated. But from the reader's point of view this is a fault only in the sense that she is too generous in her attitude toward others, too willing to do the right thing as she understands it. So, in the novel, the innocent suffer too, though not irreparably.

DAMON WILDEVE

Wildeve is looked upon by others as a man who made a good start in life but has come down. The former engineer is now the keeper of the Quiet Woman Inn, an occupation which, in many ways, suits him perfectly. Compared with Mrs. Yeobright or Clym, he is considered to be a person of little consequence. Like Eustacia, he is a hedonist, happier in the company of a woman than he is, perhaps, among men at his inn. Hardy speaks of him as the typical "man of sentiment" always yearning for the remote, "the Rousseau of Egdon."

Wildeve himself sometimes complains about his "curse of inflammability" in relation to women, but his personality is impossible to define in isolation. He finds nothing amiss in professing to love both Thomasin and Eustacia at the same time, for different reasons, of course. Unlike Eustacia's, his feelings are never deep, only easily aroused. That he is attractive to women is unquestionable, but the elements in his personality and appearance that make him so would not be attractive to men. His life style is impulsive, from his quickly responding to Eustacia's signal fire in the beginning of the novel to his unhesitating leap into the stream with all his clothes on to try to rescue Eustacia. That he dies in the attempt does not seem like a very great loss.

DIGGORY VENN

Since the reddleman is used by Hardy as the connector in developing the plot of the novel, he is hardly a character at all in the usual sense. That he is persistent, resourceful, hard-working, and prudent is clear enough, but he is so little a character in the book that it is something of a surprise to see him appear as Thomasin's suitor in Book Sixth. For all of his appearances in the story, the reader knows less about him really than about any other character. Not even his marrying Thomasin lessens the mystery, though Hardy implies in a comment about the novel that it will.

CRITICAL ANALYSIS

THEME

In this novel Hardy embodies the idea that man lives in an indifferent universe. That it might in addition be hostile to him is implied but never brought to the fore. Critics usually refer to Hardy's themes as expressing a fatalistic view of life; that is to say, a view of life which depicts human actions as subject to the control of an impersonal force, perhaps called Destiny or Fate, which is independent of both man and man's gods. The indifference of the universe, therefore, really describes what man sees as he looks about him or, perhaps, all that he can find when he is unable any longer to believe in the gods he has created. If it is said that man is created in God's image, it may also be asserted that man creates gods in his own image. The dilemma implied here is, of course, as old as man and perpetually without final answer, though historically there have been many attempted answers.

Chance and coincidence are but two ways in which this seeming indifference expresses itself in man's life. That an event is said to happen by chance or coincidence is but man's view of the matter, all he is able to see at the moment. For Hardy chance or coincidence is used as a way of showing his theme on the level of events or plot.

POINT OF VIEW

Hardy's use of point of view is conventional for his time in literary history. It can be described as a third-person or omniscient point of view. This means that events can be viewed through the eyes of whatever character at the moment suits the author's purposes. Usually, though not always, such a person is one of the main characters. Such a point of view is normally confusing to the reader only when it is shifted frequently in a short space, as, for example, in the melodramatic scenes in chapters 7-9 of Book Fifth. Following the example of Henry James, a contemporary of Hardy's, modern novelists ordinarily use a more restricted point of view, in part because of the greater reality it lends to a work of fiction. Hardy himself was no innovator of fictional techniques.

SETTING

Egdon Heath lends itself very well to the kind of story Hardy wanted to tell in the novel. It is meant as a tragedy, at least through the original five books, and the "gaunt waste" provides an appropriate setting. It is also a convenient microcosm, limited in physical extent and containing all types of human beings. Both its history and its character can be made meaningful parts of the story. Indeed, some critics go so far as to look upon Egdon as a character like any other in the novel. To do so, however, is to ignore the usual expectations the reader has of the nature of any novel.

The characters in Hardy's novel can be grouped by their attitudes toward the heath. Clym, Mrs. Yeobright, Thomasin, and Venn are products of Egdon and understand it: Clym is frequently shown, for instance, to have an intimate knowledge of its natural features; Thomasin, though well off after her husband dies, has no desire to leave it; Venn is shown to be so familiar with it that at night he can walk at full speed across it without losing his footing. On the other hand, both Eustacia and Wildeve look upon the heath as a place to flee from. It is ironical and appropriate that both should die in a stream near Shadwater Weir.

PLOT

Hardy has been criticized for his handling of plot, and it is true that like other novelists of his time he often uses chance and coincidence. This use, however, is sometimes for reasons other than simply furthering the story at a given point (see discussion under Theme). Hardy also characteristically rushes his story along at times by using a series of short scenes rather than sacrificing variety or the interest that a fast pace can maintain to the detailed development possible in a longer or long scene. It may well be that here, as in the case of his adding a sixth book, his practice is influenced by the kind of readers he knew he would have in the serial publication of his books.

Hardy's habit of using melodrama in important scenes has also been pointed out; here again he was doing nothing very different from contemporary writers. To the modern reader, however, such scenes are difficult to accept in the way he can most others in the novel, which are usually realistic and believable. The implied inconsistency here in his use of verisimilitude is itself a possible weakness in his plotting technique.

STRUCTURE

The structure of a novel is the shape given to its plot or series of events. The structure of Hardy's novel has been said to be described by a curve of expectation which traces the changes in the relationship between, and the aspirations of, Clym and Eustacia from waiting in anticipation and hope to the defeat of any possibility for happiness. This curve also reflects the changes in the relationship between the less important characters of Wildeve and Thomasin.

The structure of the novel reaches its logical completion by the end of Book Fifth; Book Sixth is an extension not accounted for by it.

SYMBOLISM

Hardy uses a number of symbols in the novel: Egdon Heath, Rainbarrow, the moon, Paris, gambling, physical impairment (eyesight), a storm, water are those singled out for comment. Many of these are aspects of the setting. Like any symbol, these are both facts and representatives of certain meanings or significance. Symbols are appropriate to a work of fiction if they can be both at the same time. They are successful if they enable an author to convey meaning without forcing it. Most of the above symbols are appropriate and successful; those which are not are connected with the melodramatic scenes at the end of Book Fifth. As with every other formal aspect of a novel, symbols help to embody an author's theme.

IRONY

Irony, the device by which in a work of literature the difference between intention and performance is shown, figures heavily in

Hardy's novel. The theme itself contains irony, it could be said. In fact, man can never know just what sort of universe he lives in; if he is convinced, for example, that the gods are indifferent to his aspirations and his life he may be wrong. In the case of Eustacia, for instance, her despair may well be caused by a mistaken view of what life is like. Hence, her view of things becomes one of the causes for her despair, though she looks upon it rather as a symptom. To take an extreme case, Hardy himself may have been quite wrong in his way of looking at life. Indeed, any view of man in relation to the universe is susceptible of irony.

STYLE

Much has been said, pro and con, about Hardy's style in his fiction. It is easy to say he has a clumsy style or an adequate style or an intermittently effective style. A demonstration of some particular aspect of his style is perhaps more useful.

Hardy's narrative style makes use of several kinds of imagery, including a number of figures of speech using analogies drawn from the setting of his story. Consider such a sampling as the following: "Eustacia's journey was at first as vague in direction as that of thistledown in the wind"; "the party had marched in trail, like a traveling flock of sheep; that is to say, the strongest first, the weak and young behind"; "[Grandfer Cantle] also began to sing, in the voice of a bee up a flue"; "Grandfer Cantle meanwhile staring at [Christian] as a hen stares at the duck she has hatched"; "in her winter dress, as now, [Eustacia] was like the tiger-beetle, which, when observed in dull situations, seems to be of the quietest neutral color, but under a full illumination blazes with dazzling splendor"; "[the settle] is, to the hearths of old-fashioned cavernous fireplaces, what the last belt of trees is to the exposed country estate, or the north wall to the garden"; "[Clym] longed for death, as a field laborer longs for the shade"; "Fairway gave a circular motion to the rope, as if he were stirring a batter"; "[Eustacia] had entered the dance from the troubled hours of her late life as one might enter a brilliant chamber after a night walk in a wood"; "the leaves of the hollyhocks hung like half-closed umbrellas." In the first of these the term carrying the analogy comes from nature; in the second, from man's daily activities on the heath In short, Hardy's imagery is appropriate to the world of his story and effective in conveying what at a given moment he wishes to show, not merely say. The examples above are but ten of more than forty figures of speech easily found in the novel, and they represent but one kind.

REVIEW QUESTIONS AND THEME TOPICS

1. Analyze the way in which Hardy presents the heath dwellers in the novel (Fairway, the Cantles, Humphrey, Sam, etc.). Include such things as personality, occupation, topics of conversation, and opinions of life and people. (See, for a start, Book First, chapter 3.)

2. Find some of the superstitions the heath dwellers believe in, and explain what these reveal about them and their view of life.

3. Several proverbs or bits of folk wisdom are pronounced by the heath folk. What kinds of truth or wisdom or even ignorance do these reveal?

4. Eustacia is said to be attractive to men. In what ways is this shown, and what does she have that Thomasin does not? (Begin with Book First, chapter 7.)

5. Develop a contrast between Clym and Wildeve as lovers and as husbands. In what specific ways are they attractive to women; in what ways, qualified to be successful husbands? (See, for example, Eustacia's comments in Book Fourth, chapter 6.)

6. Write a character sketch of either Thomasin or Wildeve. Try to include what Hardy does, for instance, in his set piece on Eustacia in Book First, chapter 7.

7. How much of a full-fledged character is Diggory Venn? In other words, analyze the way he is presented as you would with any main character, and then answer the question.

8. Analyze the kind of mother Mrs. Yeobright is by showing how she acts toward Clym, especially in situations of great stress. Her relationship to Thomasin might also be included, since she is substitute mother for the young woman. (Begin, for example, with Book Third, chapters 2 and 3, for Clym.)

9. Contrast Clym's idealism with Eustacia's romanticism. Make clear the basis on which you develop the contrast.

10. Analyze Hardy's use of foreshadowing in the plot of the novel. For instance, how does he handle the foreshadowing of Clym's eventual estrangement from his mother?

11. Collect several instances of Venn's use as a connector in the furthering of the plot; then, explain how his actions do in fact advance the story. (Begin, obviously, with Book First, chapter 2.)

12. Explain why the scenes in Book Fifth, chapters 7-9 are melodramatic by analysis of the details by which they are developed.

13. Analyze the way Hardy describes the physical setting of his novel, Egdon Heath. Look especially at the way in which he has Clym observe its natural features. (Begin with Book First, chapter 1.)

14. In Book Fourth, chapters 5-6, the heath is an active agent in Mrs. Yeobright's fate. Find another such instance in which Egdon Heath acts upon human beings, and analyze its use in the novel.

15. Trace the history of the relationship between Thomasin and Wildeve as a reflection of the structure of the novel.

16. Justify the idea that Mrs. Yeobright's death is the main point at which the curve of expectation by which the novel's structure has been described begins to fall.

17. Rainbarrow has been discussed as a symbol. Of what significance in its symbolic use is the fact that it is a Celtic burial mound? It is usually wise not to be too ingenious in literary criticism.

18. Is the fact that Venn is red in color for most of the novel of any symbolic significance? If so, explain.

19. Collect several instances of irony not already mentioned, and relate them to the theme of the novel.

20. Some of Hardy's figures of speech do not use local reference. Find several, and show what kinds of references are used to effect the analogies. If they are used for characters in the novel, explain their appropriateness.

21. What kinds of historical and/or mythological allusions does Hardy use? And when does he use them? (See, for example, Book First, chapter 7.)

22. Develop an argument, with evidences, for or against the idea that Eustacia Vye is the main character in the novel. Try to be fair in the light of Hardy's intentions.

23. Suppose you rewrote Hardy's novel so that it was told strictly from the point of view of, say, Clym. How would your novel differ from his? Be as specific as you can.

24. What would happen to his novel if you retold it from Eustacia's point of view, so that everything that happens is seen through her eyes?

25. Write an essay defending or attacking Hardy's addition of a sixth book to the original conception of five. Make clear the grounds on which you argue. Consider, for example, whether the addition was made solely to give Thomasin a happy future.

SELECTED BIBLIOGRAPHY

Abercrombie, Lascelles. *Thomas Hardy: A Critical Study*. New York, 1912. An early analysis of Hardy's work as well as a summary of his attitudes.

Beach, Joseph Warren. *The Technique of Thomas Hardy*. Chicago, 1922. A study of the "structural art" of Hardy's novels, major and minor.

Guerard, Albert J. *Thomas Hardy: The Novels and Stories*. Cambridge, Mass., 1949. A study of Hardy's novels whose main purpose is "to describe the content and accomplishment of his novels in the simplest possible terms."

————— (ed.). *Hardy: A Collection of Critical Essays.* Englewood Cliffs, N.J., 1963. Essays on Hardy's art, his major novels, his characters, and his poetry by such writers as D. H. Lawrence, John Holloway, Albert Guerard, Dorothy Van Ghent, and Samuel Hynes.

Hardy, Florence E. *The Early Life of Thomas Hardy.* London, 1928. A biography by Hardy's second wife, which was probably planned and partly written by Hardy himself.

—————. *The Later Years of Thomas Hardy.* London, 1930. See Hardy, above.

Rutland, William. *Thomas Hardy: A Study of His Writings and Their Background.* Oxford, 1938. A study of the intellectual background of Hardy's thought and writing.

The Southern Review (Thomas Hardy Centennial Issue), Vol. VI (Summer 1940). Essays on various aspects of Hardy's fiction and poetry by such writers as R. P. Blackmur, F. R. Leavis, Arthur Mizener, John Crowe Ransom, and Allen Tate; those by Donald Davidson, Morton Dauwen Zabel, Delmore Schwartz, and W. H. Auden are reprinted in the collection edited by Guerard (listed above).

Weber, Carl J. *Hardy of Wessex: His Life and Literary Career.* New York, 1940. A study of Hardy's life and career, a second edition of which appeared in 1965, making use of recent scholarship and additional information from letters.

Webster, Harvey C. *On a Darkling Plain.* Chicago, 1947. A study of "the evolution of Hardy's thought and its effect upon his art."

NOTES